Erstes Englisch
mit Billy Malone

Das Bildwörterbuch

Erste Wörter und Sätze

Von Birgit Fuchs
Illustriert von Manfred Tophoven

TESSLOFF

Foreword

Vorwort

Herzlich willkommen in der Welt von Billy Malone!
Auf den nächsten Seiten lernst du Billy und seine Familie kennen und entdeckst, wie die Familie Malone lebt. Gleichzeitig lernst du viele wichtige und nützliche englische Wörter und übst deine ersten englischen Sätze.

Und so kannst du mit diesem Bildwörterbuch üben:
In den **Bildern** auf jeder Seite findest du Beschriftungen vieler Gegenstände in Englisch und Deutsch. So kannst du dir die Vokabeln zu den einzelnen Themen leicht einprägen. In den **Randspalten** findest du noch mehr Bilder und Vokabeln, die deinen Wortschatz ergänzen können. **Billy's basics** beinhalten einfache englische Grammatik für einen allerersten Überblick. Und schließlich erfährst du unter der Rubrik **Make sentences**, wie du mit den Wörtern, die du gelernt hast, deine ersten englischen Sätze bilden kannst.

Am besten lernst du Englisch, wenn du so viel wie möglich sprichst! Vielleicht lässt du dir die englischen Wörter von jemandem vorlesen, der Englisch kann. Oder du hörst dir die richtige Aussprache im Internet auf **www.tessloff.com** an. Dort werden dir die Vokabeln jedes Kapitels vorgelesen.

Damit man genau weiß, wie die Wörter ausgesprochen werden, gibt es die so genannte **Lautschrift.** Sie benutzt bestimmte Zeichen, die immer für einen ganz bestimmten Laut stehen. Im Vokabelverzeichnis am Ende des Buches findest du hinter jedem englischen Wort auch die dazugehörige Lautschrift.

Dies sind die wichtigsten Zeichen:

ɑː wie in lahm
iː wie in Biene
uː wie in Blume
i wie in Baby
ɪ wie in Kiste
e wie in Bett
æ ähnlich wie in Bär
ʌ wie in Kamm
ɒ wie in Motte
ə wie in Mitte
ʊ wie in Butter

aɪ wie in Mai
ɔɪ wie in Eule
aʊ wie in Haus
eə ähnlich wie in leer
ɪə wie in Tier
ɜː ähnlich wie in hört
ʤ wie in Dschungel
ʒ wie in Garage
ŋ wie in Ring
ʃ wie in Schlange
ʧ wie in tschüss

v wie in Vase
z wie in Sonne
s wie in Messer

Diese Laute gibt es nur in Englisch:

θ wie in think
ð wie in this
w wie in water
r wie in red
eɪ wie in day
əʊ wie in low

Contents

Inhalt

Numbers from 1 to 100

Zahlen von 1 bis 100

1	2	3	4	5
one	two	three	four	five
11	12	13	14	15
eleven	twelve	thirteen	fourteen	fifteen
21	22	23	24	25
twenty-one	twenty-two	twenty-three	twenty-four	twenty-five
31	32	33	34	35
thirty-one	thirty-two	thirty-three	thirty-four	thirty-five
41	42	43	44	45
forty-one	forty-two	forty-three	forty-four	forty-five
51	52	53	54	55
fifty-one	fifty-two	fifty-three	fifty-four	fifty-five
61	62	63	64	65
sixty- one	sixty-two	sixty-three	sixty-four	sixty-five
71	72	73	74	75
seventy-one	seventy-two	seventy-three	seventy-four	seventy-five
81	82	83	84	85
eighty-one	eighty-two	eighty-three	eighty-four	eighty-five
91	92	93	94	95
ninety-one	ninety-two	ninety-three	ninety-four	ninety-five

6	7	8	9	10
six	seven	eight	nine	ten
16	17	18	19	20
sixteen	seventeen	eighteen	nineteen	twenty
26	27	28	29	30
twenty-six	twenty-seven	twenty-eight	twenty-nine	thirty
36	37	38	39	40
thirty-six	thirty-seven	thirty-eight	thirty-nine	forty
46	47	48	49	50
forty-six	forty-seven	forty-eight	forty-nine	fifty
56	57	58	59	60
fifty-six	fifty-seven	fifty-eight	fifty-nine	sixty
66	67	68	69	70
sixty-six	sixty-seven	sixty-eight	sixty-nine	seventy
76	77	78	79	80
seventy-six	seventy-seven	seventy-eight	seventy-nine	eighty
86	87	88	89	90
eighty-six	eighty-seven	eighty-eight	eighty-nine	ninety
96	97	98	99	100
ninety-six	ninety-seven	ninety-eight	ninety-nine	a hundred

The Malones, Billy's family

Die Malones, Billys Familie

Mary, Billy's mother
Mary, Billys Mutter
und
Susan, Billy's baby sister
Susan, Billys kleine Schwester

Laura, Billy's grandmother
Laura, Billys Großmutter

Peter, Billy's father
Peter, Billys Vater

Joe, Billy's grandfather
Joe, Billys Großvater

Tom, Billy's uncle
Tom, Billys Onkel

Claire, Billy's aunt
Claire, Billys Tante

Peggy, Billy's cousin
Peggy, Billys Cousine

Charly, Billy's dog
Charly, Billys Hund

Billy

Sally, Billy's sister
Sally, Billys Schwester

Ron, Billy's cousin
Ron, Billys Cousin

Billy's basics

I	– ich
you	– du
he, she, it	– er, sie, es
we	– wir
you	– ihr
they	– sie

I am (I'm)	– ich bin
you are (you're)	– du bist
he, she, it is (he's, she's, it's)	– er, sie, es ist
we are (we're)	– wir sind
you are (you're)	– ihr seid
they are (they're)	– sie sind

parents
Eltern

adults
Erwachsene

woman
Frau

wife
Ehefrau

man
Mann

husband
Ehemann

boy
Junge

son
Sohn

brother
Bruder

girl
Mädchen

daughter
Tochter

sister
Schwester

child
Kind

children
Kinder

Make sentences!

I'm Billy. I'm Sally's brother.
Ich bin Billy. Ich bin Sallys Bruder.

I'm Mary. I'm Peter's wife.
Ich bin Mary. Ich bin Peters Frau.

This is Mary. She is Billy's mother.
Das ist Mary. Sie ist Billys Mutter.

I'm Sally. I'm Mary's daughter.
Ich bin Sally. Ich bin Marys Tochter.

The Malones' house

Das Haus der Malones

book
Buch

ball
Ball

watering can
Gießkanne

helicopter
Hubschrauber

tree
Baum

Billy's basics

on	– auf	in front of	– vor
under	– unter	between	– zwischen
behind	– hinter	next to	– neben
over	– über		

Make sentences!

Where is the balloon? Wo ist der Ballon?	The balloon is over the garage. Der Ballon ist über der Garage.
Where is the book? Wo ist das Buch?	The book is on the bench. Das Buch ist auf der Bank.

In the garden
Im Garten

leaf
Blatt

grass
Gras

sun
Sonne

sunflower
Sonnenblume

rose
Rose

Billy's basics

I can see	– ich kann sehen	we can see	– wir können sehen
you can see	– du kannst sehen	you can see	– ihr könnt sehen
he, she, it can see	– er, sie, es kann sehen	they can see	– sie können sehen

a (an) – ein, eine   the – der, die, das

bee
Biene

butterfly
Schmetterling

fly
Fliege

ant
Ameise

spider
Spinne

beetle
Käfer

Make sentences!

I can see the sun.
Ich kann die Sonne sehen.

I can see the grass.
Ich kann das Gras sehen.

I can see a butterfly.
Ich kann einen Schmetterling sehen.

I can see an ant.
Ich kann eine Ameise sehen.

In the living room

Im Wohnzimmer

candle
Kerze

vase
Vase

newspaper
Zeitung

magazine
Zeitschrift

budgie
Wellensittich

Billy's basics

I am looking for	– ich suche	we are looking for	– wir suchen
you are looking for	– du suchst	you are looking for	– ihr sucht
he, she, it is looking for	– er, sie, es sucht	they are looking for	– sie suchen

Make sentences!

Billy is looking for the book.
Billy sucht das Buch.

Sally is looking for the magazine.
Sally sucht die Zeitschrift.

In the kitchen
In der Küche

pot
Topf

cup
Tasse

plate
Teller

glass
Glas

knife
Messer

Billy's basics

Look, there is ... – Schau, da ist / da gibt es ...
Look, there are ... – Schau, da sind ...

saucer
Untertasse

fork
Gabel

spoon
Löffel

bowl
Schüssel

pan
Pfanne

bottle
Flasche

Make sentences!

Look, there is a plate on the table!
Schau, da ist ein Teller auf dem Tisch!

Look, there are cups in the cupboard!
Schau, da sind Tassen im Schrank!

In the children's room

Im Kinderzimmer

football
Fußball

umbrella
Regenschirm

teddy bear
Teddybär

doll
Puppe

Billy's basics

I have got	– ich habe	I (ich)	– my (mein)
you have got	– du hast	you (du)	– your (dein)
he, she, it has got	– er, sie, es hat	he, she, it (er, sie, es)	– his, her, its (sein, ihr, sein)
we have got	– wir haben	we (wir)	– our (unser)
you have got	– ihr habt	you (ihr)	– your (euer)
they have got	– sie haben	they (sie)	– their (ihr)

toy car
Spielzeugauto

clock
Uhr

skipping rope
Hüpfseil

pencil
Bleistift

glove puppet
Handpuppe

Make sentences!

I've got a dog. It's my dog.
Ich habe einen Hund. Es ist mein Hund.

We've got a picture book.
Wir haben ein Bilderbuch.

It's our picture book.
Es ist unser Bilderbuch.

She's got a ball. It's her ball.
Sie hat einen Ball. Es ist ihr Ball.

They've got a computer.
Sie haben einen Computer.

It's their computer.
Es ist ihr Computer.

In the bathroom

Im Badezimmer

soap
Seife

comb
Kamm

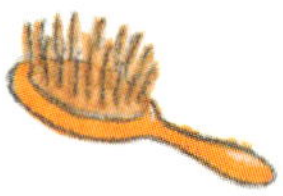

hairbrush
Haarbürste

toothbrush
Zahnbürste

toothpaste
Zahncreme

Billy's basics

red	– rot	black	– schwarz
blue	– blau	grey	– grau
green	– grün	purple	– lila
yellow	– gelb	orange	– orange
pink	– rosa	brown	– braun

fish
Fisch

duck
Ente

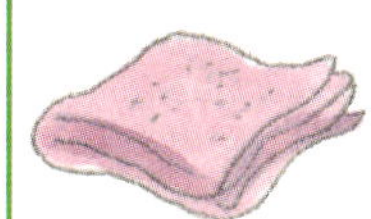
towel
Handtuch

hair-dryer
Föhn

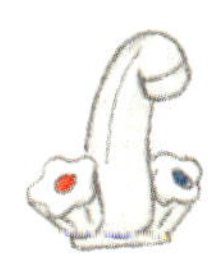
tap
Wasserhahn

sponge
Schwamm

Make sentences!

What colour is the soap? The soap is green.
Welche Farbe hat die Seife? Die Seife ist grün.
What colour is the towel? The towel is pink.
Welche Farbe hat das Handtuch? Das Handtuch ist rosa.

My body
Mein Körper

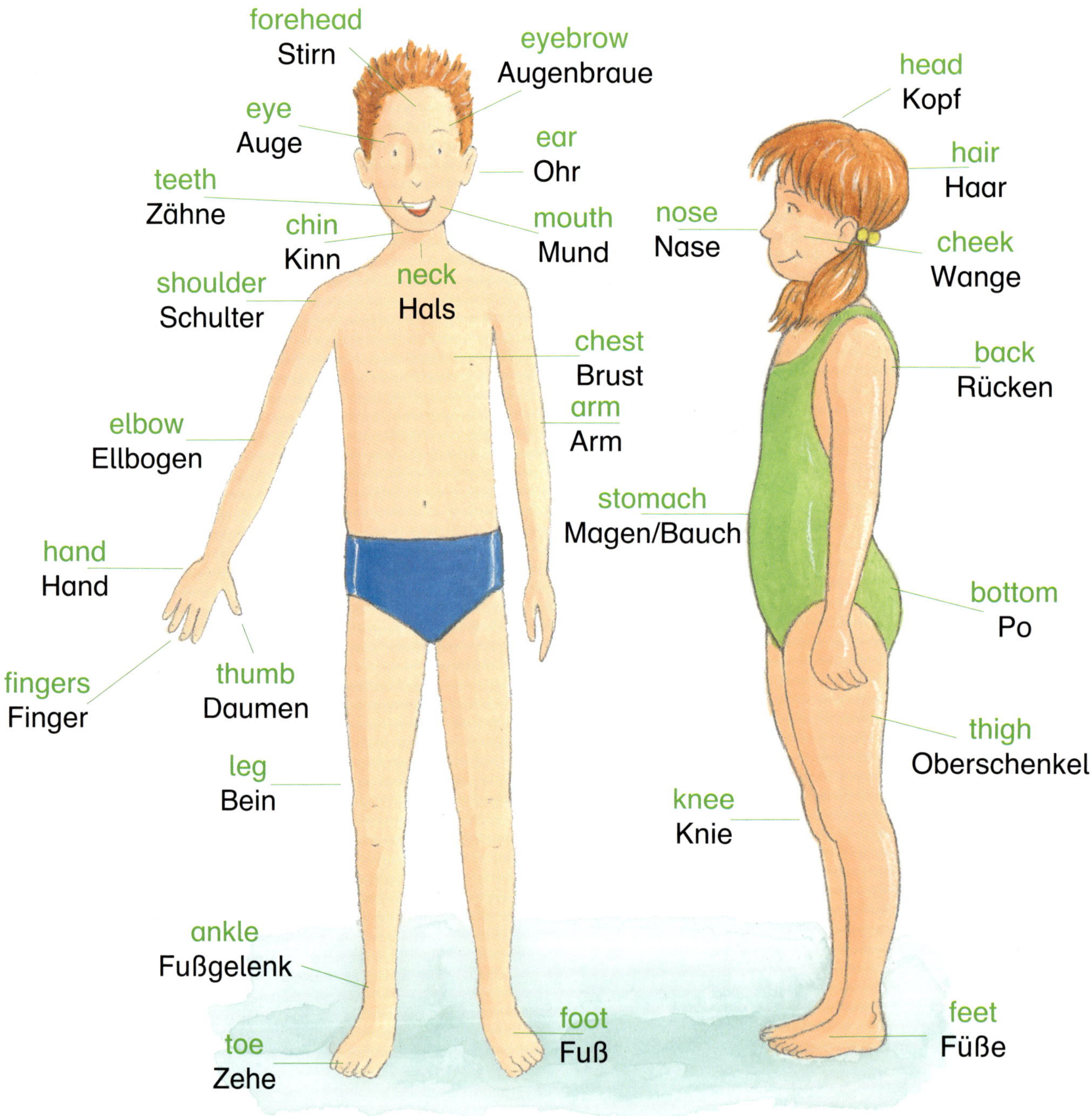

Billy's basics

It is called... – Es wird ... genannt.
This part is called... – Dieser Teil wird ... genannt.
This part of the body... – Dieser Teil des Körpers...

cartwheel
Rad

knee bend
Kniebeuge

headstand
Kopfstand

handstand
Handstand

back bend
Brücke

one-leg stand
Waage

forward roll
Rolle vorwärts

backward roll
Rolle rückwärts

Make sentences!

This part of the body is called the knee.
Dieser Teil des Körpers wird Knie genannt.

I can do a headstand.
Ich kann einen Kopfstand machen.

Clothes

Kleidung

Billy's basics

it is (it's)	– es ist …
it is not (it isn't)	– es ist nicht … / es ist kein …
this is	– dies ist …
this isn't	– das ist nicht … / das ist kein …
these are	– dies sind …
these aren't	– das sind nicht … / das sind keine …

Make sentences!

It's a dress. It isn't a skirt.
Es ist ein Kleid. Es ist kein Rock.

This is a skirt. This isn't a bag.
Das ist ein Rock. Das ist keine Tasche.

At school

In der Schule

chalk
Kreide

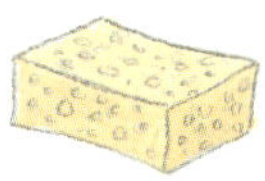

sponge
Schwamm

exercise book
Heft

pencil sharpener
Anspitzer

pen
Füller

TIME	MONDAY	TUESDAY	WEDNESDAY	THURSDAY	FRIDAY
9.00	Maths Mathe	English Englisch	Maths Mathe	English Englisch	General Studies Sachkunde
9.50	Reading Lesen	Reading Lesen	PE Sport	Reading Lesen	English Englisch
10.30	Break Pause	Break Pause	Break Pause	Break Pause	Break Pause
10.50	Music Musik	Maths Mathe	English Englisch	German Deutsch	Maths Mathe
11.40	English Englisch	French Französisch	English Englisch	Religious Education Religion	Maths Mathe
12.20	Lunch Mittag-essen	Lunch Mittag-essen	Lunch Mittag-essen	Lunch Mittag-essen	Lunch Mittag-essen
1.00	Science Natur-wissenschaft	General Studies Sachkunde	Art Kunst	Science Natur-wissenschaft	Reading Lesen
2.00	Physical Education Sport	Religious Education Religion	Reading Lesen	Maths Mathe	Science Natur-wissenschaft
3.00	HOME	HOME	HOME	HOME	HOME

Billy's basics

1. first – der / die / das Erste; erstens
2. second – der / die / das Zweite; zweitens
3. third – der / die / das Dritte; drittens
4. fourth – der / die / das Vierte; viertens
5. fifth – der / die / das Fünfte; fünftens
6. sixth – der / die / das Sechste; sechstens

Make sentences!

On Monday we've got six lessons.
Am Montag haben wir sechs Unterrichtsstunden.

The first lesson is maths.
Die erste Unterrichtsstunde ist Mathe.

Animals
Tiere

dolphin
Delfin

peacock
Pfau

flamingo
Flamingo

tiger
Tiger

fox
Fuchs

duck
Ente

budgie
Wellensittich

guinea pig
Meerschweinchen

rhino
Nashorn

fish
Fisch

crocodile
Krokodil

hippo
Flusspferd

snake
Schlange

hamster
Hamster

turtle
Schildkröte

penguin
Pinguin

rabbit
Kaninchen

zebra
Zebra

Billy's basics

Do you know ... ? – Weißt du ...? / Kennst du ...?

bear
Bär

hedgehog
Igel

mouse
Maus

wolf
Wolf

giraffe
Giraffe

dog
Hund

parrot
Papagei

elephant
Elefant

polar bear
Eisbär

beaver
Biber

eagle
Adler

bird
Vogel

hare
Hase

cat
Katze

monkey
Affe

lion
Löwe

kangaroo
Känguru

Make sentences!

Do you know what this animal is called?
Weißt du, wie dieses Tier heißt?

This is a bear.
Das ist ein Bär.

On the farm

Auf dem Bauernhof

pig
Schwein

goat
Ziege

sheep
Schaf

hen
Henne

cock
Hahn

Billy's basics

how many – wie viele
How many things can you see? – Wie viele Dinge kannst du sehen?

horse
Pferd

chick
Küken

duck
Ente

cow
Kuh

dog
Hund

farmer
Bauer

Make sentences!

How many cows can you see?
Wie viele Kühe kannst du sehen?

I can see two cows.
Ich kann zwei Kühe sehen.

Food
Lebensmittel

peach
Pfirsich

tomato
Tomate

grapes
Weintrauben

apple
Apfel

honey
Honig

orange
Apfelsine

pineapple
Ananas

tomato
Tomate

lettuce
Salat

peach
Pfirsich

cucumber
Gurke

cauliflower
Blumenkohl

strawberries
Erdbeeren

apple
Apfel

potatoes
Kartoffeln

grapes
Weintrauben

banana
Banane

peas
Erbsen

beans
Bohnen

plums
Pflaumen

sweetcorn
Mais

cherries
Kirschen

mushrooms
Pilze

pear
Birne

lemon
Zitrone

red pepper
roter Paprika

carrot
Möhre

Billy's basics

Can I have ..., please?	– Kann ich bitte ... haben?
Thank you.	– Danke.
Yes, you can. Here you are.	– Ja, hier bitte.
You're welcome.	– Bitte schön.

cake
Kuchen

biscuits
Kekse

milk
Milch

lemonade
Limonade

chewing gum
Kaugummi

chocolate
Schokolade

vinegar
Essig

oil
Öl

tea
Tee

eggs
Eier

orange juice
Orangensaft

coffee
Kaffee

cocoa
Kakao

jam
Marmelade

ham
Schinken

bread
Brot

butter
Butter

cheese
Käse

salt
Salz

pepper
Pfeffer

sugar
Zucker

sausages
Würstchen

honey
Honig

sausages
Würstchen

chips
Pommes frites

chewing gum
Kaugummi

lemonade
Limonade

chocolate
Schokolade

Make sentences!

Can I have a banana, please?
Kann ich bitte eine Banane haben?

Yes, you can. Here you are.
Ja, bitte schön.

Can I have some milk, please?
Kann ich bitte etwas Milch haben?

Thank you. You're welcome.
Danke. Bitte schön.

In town

In der Stadt

bicycle
Fahrrad

bus
Bus

fire engine
Feuerwehrauto

bus stop
Bushaltestelle

car
Auto

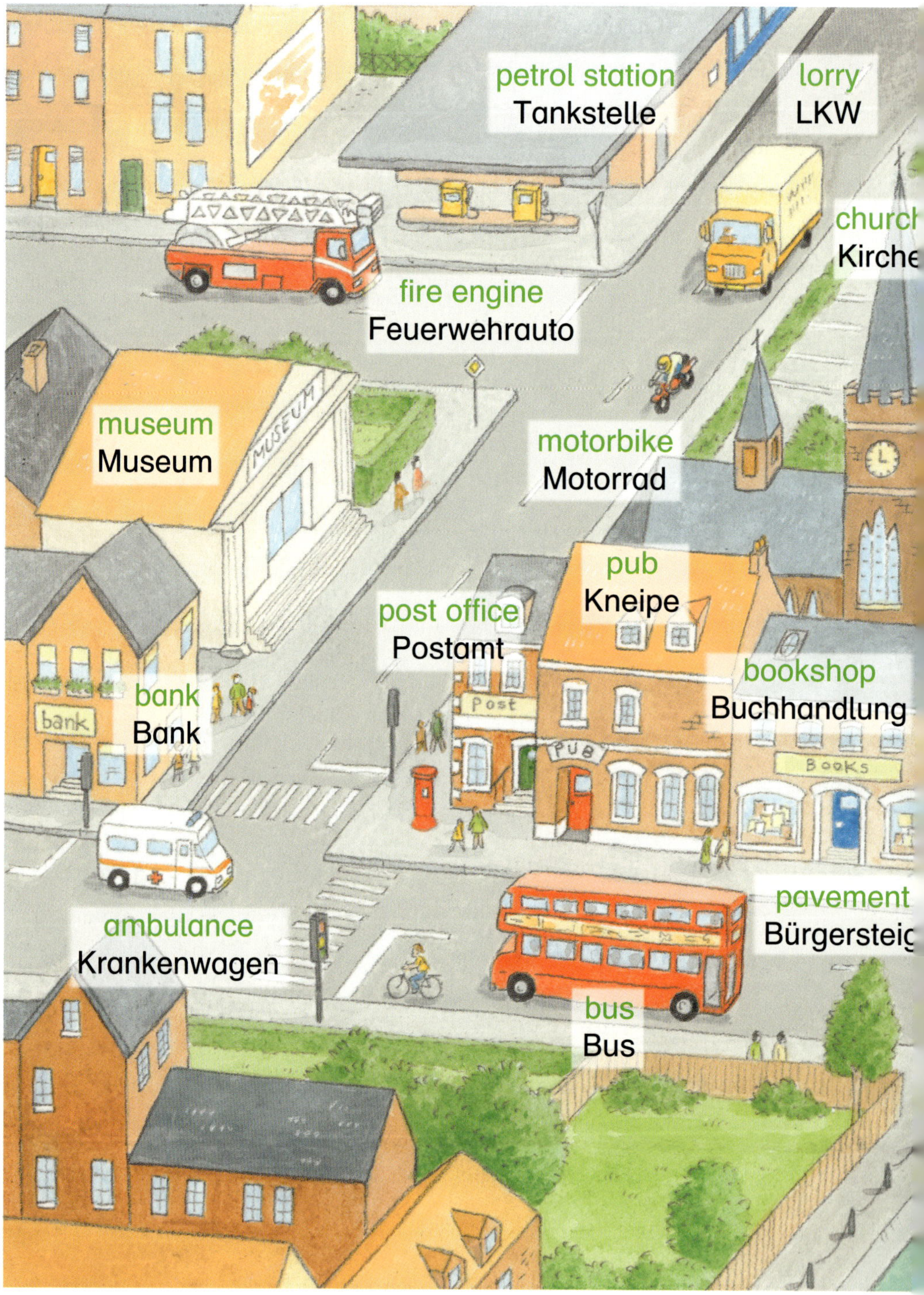

Billy's basics

on the left – links

on the right – rechts

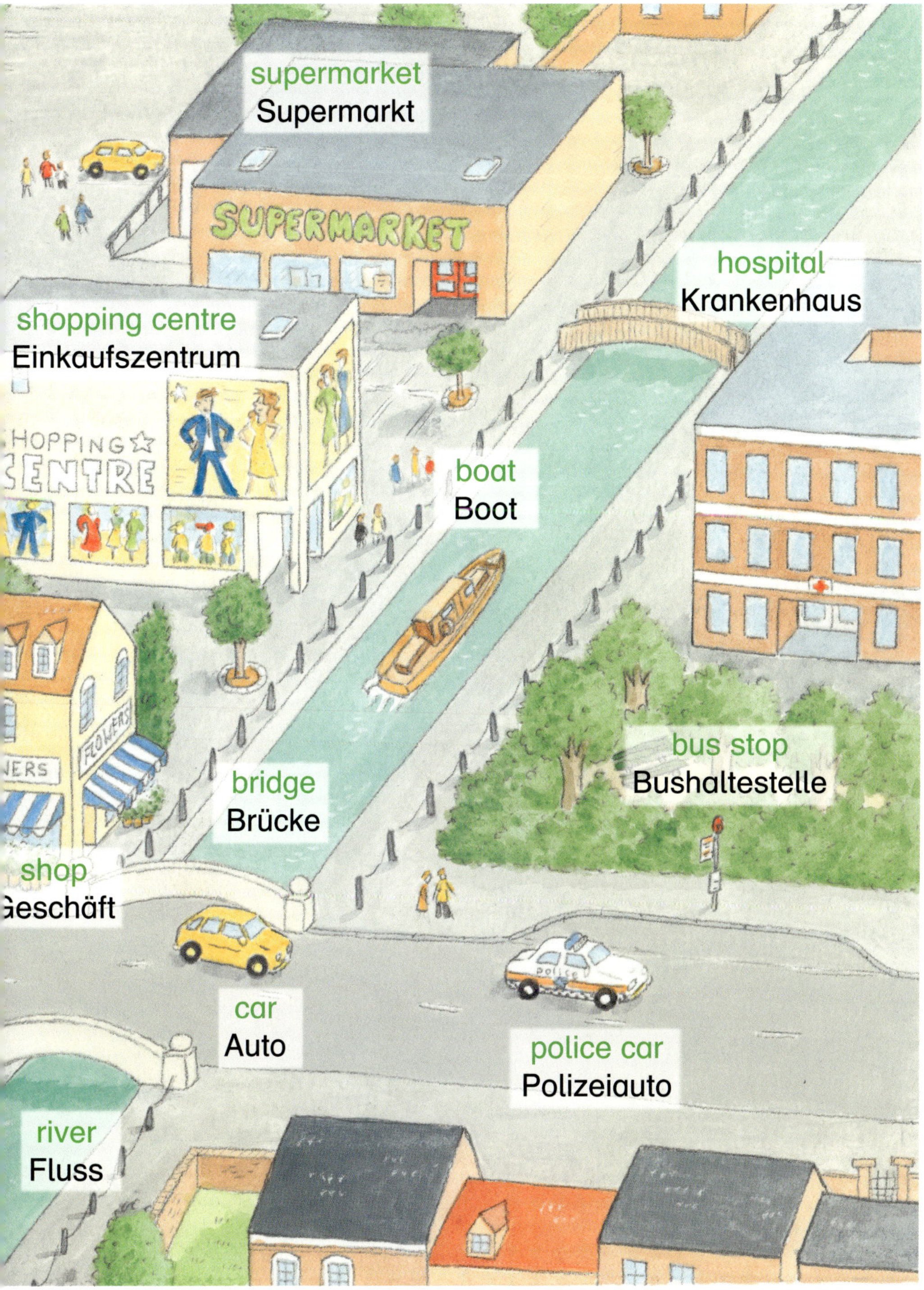

ambulance
Krankenwagen

traffic lights
Ampel

motorbike
Motorrad

lorry
LKW

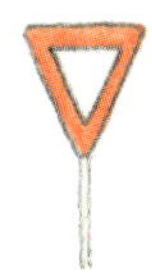

traffic sign
Verkehrsschild

police car
Polizeiauto

Make sentences!

On the left you can see a church.
Links kannst du eine Kirche sehen.

On the right there is a park.
Rechts ist ein Park.

Opposites

Gegensätze

Billy's basics

but	– aber
the opposite of	– das Gegenteil von

Susan

happy
glücklich

Sally

sad
traurig

closed
geschlossen

door
Tür

open
geöffnet

window
Fenster

Billy

Susan

loud
laut

quiet
leise

butterfly
Schmetterling

toad
Kröte

ugly
hässlich

beautiful
schön

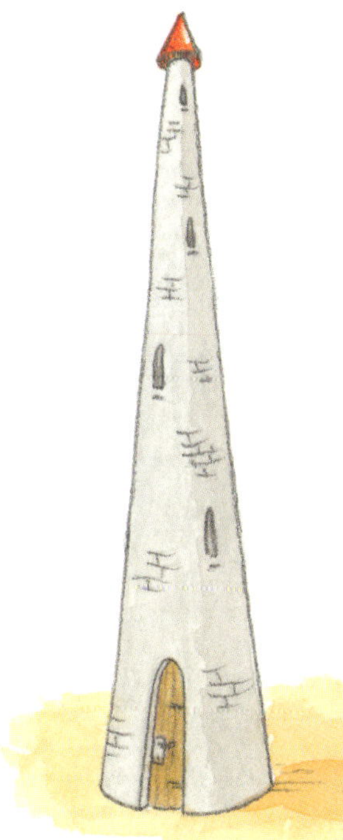

tower
Turm

high
hoch

house
Haus

low
niedrig

stone
Stein

hard
hart

feather
Feder

soft
weich

Make sentences!

The cat is fat, but Charly is thin.
Die Katze ist dick, aber Charly ist dünn.

The opposite of fat is thin.
Das Gegenteil von dick ist dünn.

What is Billy doing?

Was macht Billy gerade?

to smile
lächeln

to whisper
flüstern

to write
schreiben

to sleep
schlafen

to sing
singen

to dream
träumen

to eat
essen

to run
rennen

to cry
weinen

to wait
warten

to jump
springen

to read
lesen

to kiss
küssen

to drink
trinken

to talk
reden

to swing
schaukeln

Billy's basics

to sing	– singen	we are singing	– wir singen gerade
I am singing	– ich singe gerade	you are singing	– ihr singt gerade
you are singing	– du singst gerade	they are singing	– sie singen gerade
he, she, it is singing	– er, sie, es singt gerade		

to paint
malen

to clean
putzen

to think
denken

to push
drücken

to climb
klettern

to pull
ziehen

to sit
sitzen

to draw
zeichnen

to walk
gehen

to give
geben

to take
nehmen

to knock
klopfen

to listen
zuhören

to show
zeigen

to carry
tragen

to shout
rufen

Make sentences!

Billy is laughing.
Billy lacht gerade.

Billy is running.
Billy rennt gerade.

Billy is painting.
Billy malt gerade.

Billy is waiting.
Billy wartet gerade.

At the fair

Auf dem Jahrmarkt

balloon
Ballon

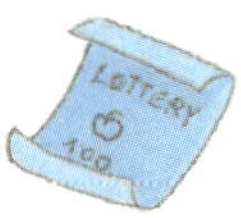

ticket
Los

ticket
Eintrittskarte

plastic flower
Plastikblume

candy floss
Zuckerwatte

Billy's basics

How much is ...?	– Wie viel kostet ...?
How much are ...?	– Wie viel kosten ...?

chips
Pommes frites

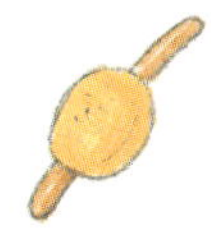

hot dog
Hotdog

hamburger
Hamburger

ice cream
Eis

popcorn
Popcorn

Coke
Cola

Make sentences!

How much is a ticket for the roller coaster? It costs .... pounds.
Was kostet eine Karte für die Achterbahn? Sie kostet ... Pfund.

The Malones are very busy

Die Malones sind sehr beschäftigt

Billy's basics

six o'clock	– sechs Uhr (6.00 Uhr)
half past nine	– halb zehn (9.30 Uhr)
a quarter past seven	– Viertel nach sieben (7.15 Uhr)
a quarter to one	– Viertel vor eins (12.45 Uhr)
a.m.	– morgens (0.00 bis 12.00)
p.m.	– abends (12.00 bis 0.00)

Make sentences!

At six o'clock Susan wakes up.
Um sechs Uhr wacht Susan auf.

At half past four Billy plays football.
Um halb fünf spielt Billy Fußball.

At the swimming pool
Im Schwimmbad

life belt
Rettungsring

beach ball
Wasserball

diving rings
Tauchringe

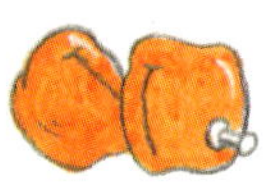

water wings
Schwimmflügel

lilo
Luftmatratze

Billy's basics

Let's go to .... – Lass uns zum ... gehen.
Let's play with .... – Lass uns mit ... spielen.

rubber ring
Schwimmring

water slide
Wasserrutsche

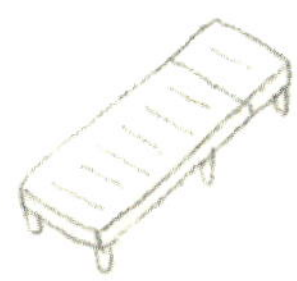

sun lounger
Sonnenliege

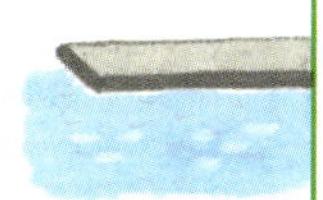

diving board
Sprungbrett

starting block
Startblock

pool
Becken

Make sentences!

Let's go to the pool!
Lass uns zum Schwimmbecken gehen!

Let's play with the diving-rings!
Lass uns mit den Tauchringen spielen!

Sport
Sport

swimming
Schwimmen

ice-skating
Eislauf

volleyball
Volleyball

riding
Reiten

badminton
Badminton

tennis
Tennis

rowing
Rudern

golf
Golf

gymnastics
Turnen

skating
Skaten

ice hockey
Eishockey

surfing
Surfen

Billy's basics

I like	– ich mag	I don't like	– ich mag nicht
you like	– du magst	you don't like	– du magst nicht
he, she, it likes	– er, sie, es mag	he, she, it doesn't like	– er, sie, es mag nicht
we like	– wir mögen	we don't like	– wir mögen nicht
you like	– ihr mögt	you don't like	– ihr mögt nicht
they like	– sie mögen	they don't like	– sie mögen nicht

cross-country skiing
Skilanglauf

basketball
Basketball

jogging
Joggen

water-skiing
Wasserski

snowboarding
Snowboarden

football / soccer
Fußball

sailing
Segeln

downhill
Abfahrt (Ski)

bobsleighing
Bob fahren

weightlifting
Gewichtheben

dancing
Tanzen

cycling
Radsport

Make sentences!

I like volleyball.
Ich mag Volleyball.

She doesn't like tennis.
Sie mag kein Tennis.

Do you like surfing? Yes, I do.
Magst du surfen? Ja.

Do you like dancing? No, I don't.
Magst du Tanzen? Nein.

At the campsite

Auf dem Zeltplatz

Billy's basics

to give – geben
Give me ..., please. – Gib mir ..., bitte

hiking boots
Wanderstiefel

bellows
Blasebalg

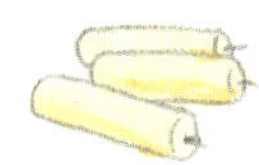

candles
Kerzen

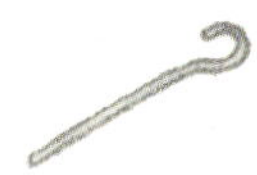

tent peg
Hering

rope
Leine

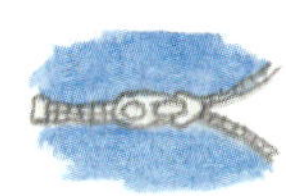

zip
Reißverschluss

Make sentences!

Give me the cushion, please.
Gib mir das Kissen, bitte.

Give me the torch, please.
Gib mir die Taschenlampe, bitte.

At the doctor's
Beim Arzt

gargle
Gurgelmittel

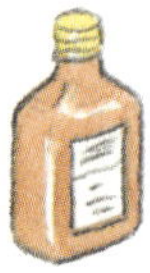

cold compress
kalte Kompresse

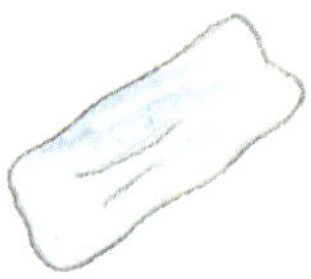

thermometer
Thermometer

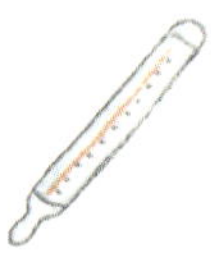

cough medicine
Hustensaft

hot-water bottle
Wärmflasche

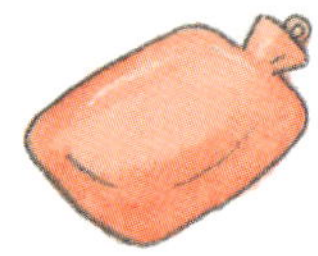

handkerchief
Taschentuch

foot bath
Fußbad

tablets
Tabletten

Billy's basics

I need	– ich brauche	we need	– wir brauchen
you need	– du brauchst	you need	– ihr braucht
he, she, it needs	– er, sie, es braucht	they need	– sie brauchen

plaster
Gips

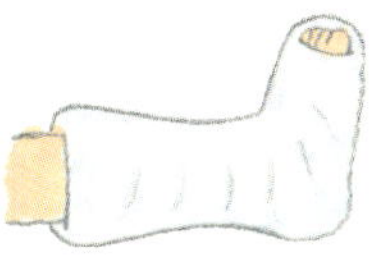

glasses
Brille

hearing aid
Hörgerät

dentist
Zahnarzt

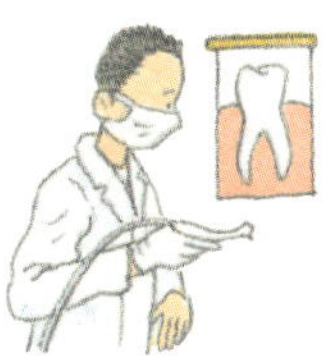

plaster
Pflaster

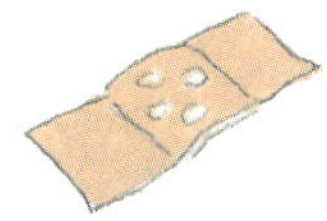

bandage
Verband

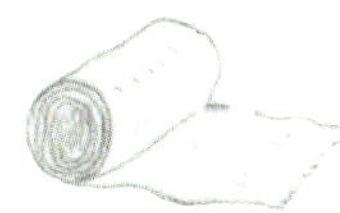

ointment
Salbe

injection
Spritze

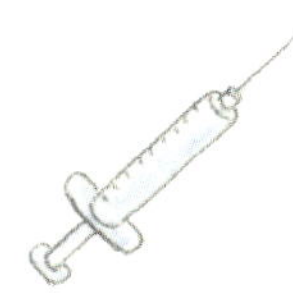

Make sentences!

Tom has a fracture. He needs a plaster.
Tom hat einen Knochenbruch. Er braucht einen Gips.

Professions

Berufe

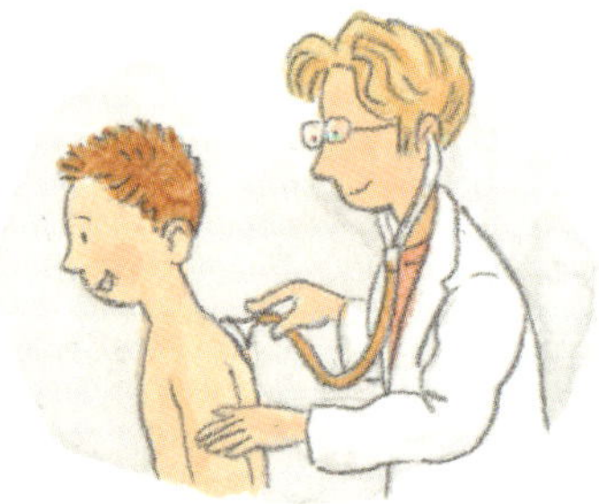

doctor
Arzt

baker
Bäcker

hairdresser
Friseur

computer programmer
Programmierer

dentist
Zahnarzt

astronaut
Astronaut

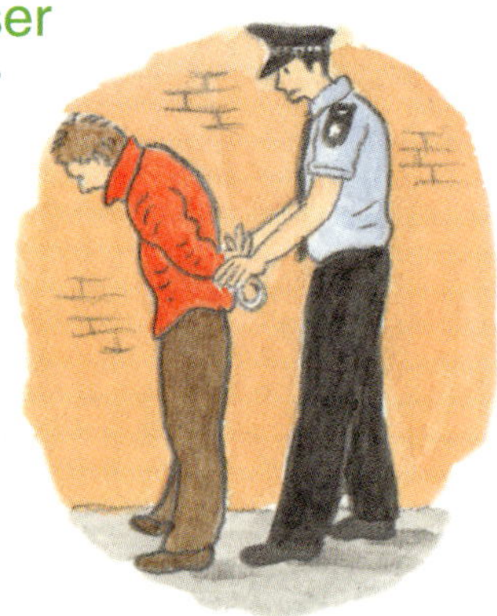

policeman
Polizist

singer
Sängerin

painter and decorator
Maler und Anstreicher

chef
Koch

Billy's basics

When I'm older … – Wenn ich älter bin …
When I'm grown up … – Wenn ich erwachsen bin …
I want to be … – Ich will … werden.

teacher
Lehrerin

butcher
Fleischer

farmer
Bauer

dancer
Tänzer

fireman
Feuerwehrmann

tailor
Schneider

postman
Postbote

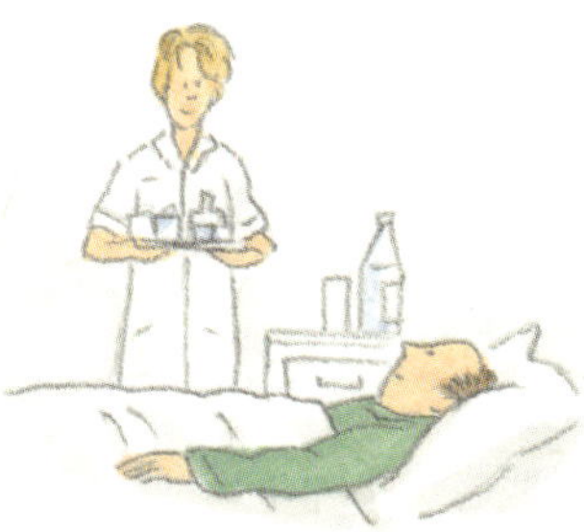

nurse
Krankenschwester

manager
Manager

vet
Tierarzt

Make sentences!

When I'm older,
I want to be a singer.
Wenn ich älter bin,
will ich Sänger werden.

When I'm grown up,
I want to be a teacher.
Wenn ich erwachsen bin,
will ich Lehrer werden.

The weather
Das Wetter

Billy's basics

rain	– Regen	cloud	– Wolke	It's raining.
snow	– Schnee	sky	– Himmel	Es regnet.
wind	– Wind	sun	– Sonne	It's snowing.
storm	– Sturm	thunder	– Donner	Es schneit.
fog	– Nebel	lightning	– Blitz	It's hailing.
hail	– Hagel	thunderstorm	– Gewitter	Es hagelt.

Make sentences!

What's the weather like today?
Wie ist das Wetter heute?

It's foggy today.
Heute ist es neblig.

What's the weather like today?
Wie ist das Wetter heute?

It's hailing today.
Heute hagelt es.

The year and the seasons

Das Jahr und die Jahreszeiten

Billy's basics

January	– Januar	May	– Mai	September	– September
February	– Februar	June	– Juni	October	– Oktober
March	– März	July	– Juli	November	– November
April	– April	August	– August	December	– Dezember

Make sentences!

In January Billy builds a snowman.
Im Januar baut Billy einen Schneemann.

In summer Sally swims in the lake.
Im Sommer schwimmt Sally im See.

Vocabulary

Vokabeln

A

a [ə]	ein, eine
ache [eɪk]	Schmerz
adult ['ædʌlt]	Erwachsener
air mattress ['eəˌmætrəs]	Luftmatratze
alphabet ['ælfəbet]	Alphabet
ambulance ['æmbjʊləns]	Krankenwagen
animal ['ænɪməl]	Tier
ankle ['æŋkl]	Fußgelenk
ant [ænt]	Ameise
apple ['æpl]	Apfel
apple tree ['æplˌtriː]	Apfelbaum
April ['eɪprəl]	April
arm [ɑːm]	Arm
armchair ['ɑːmtʃeə]	Sessel
art [ɑːt]	Kunst
astronaut ['æstrənɔːt]	Astronaut, Astronautin
at home [ət 'həʊm]	zu Hause
August ['ɔːgəst]	August
aunt [ɑːnt]	Tante
autumn ['ɔːtəm]	Herbst

B

baby, babies ['beɪbi]	Baby, Babys
back [bæk]	Rücken
backache ['bækeɪk]	Rückenschmerzen
back bend ['bækˌbend]	Brücke (Gymnastik)
backward roll ['bækwəd ˌrəʊl]	Rolle rückwärts
badminton ['bædmɪntən]	Badminton
bag [bæg]	Tasche
to bake [beɪk]	backen
baker ['beɪkə]	Bäcker, Bäckerin
balcony ['bælkəni]	Balkon
ball [bɔːl]	Ball
balloon [bə'luːn]	Ballon
banana [bə'nɑːnə]	Banane
bandage ['bændɪdʒ]	Verband
bank [bæŋk]	Bank
barn [bɑːn]	Scheune
basics ['beɪsɪks]	Grundlagen
basin ['beɪsn]	Waschbecken
basketball ['bɑːskɪtbɔːl]	Basketball
bath [bɑːθ]	Badewanne
bathmat ['bɑːθmæt]	Badematte
bathrobe ['bɑːθrəʊb]	Bademantel
bathroom ['bɑːθrʊm]	Badezimmer
beach ball ['biːtʃˌbɔːl]	Wasserball
bean [biːn]	Bohne
bear [beə]	Bär
beautiful ['bjuːtɪfʊl]	schön
beaver ['biːvə]	Biber
bed [bed]	Bett
bee [biː]	Biene
beetle ['biːtl]	Käfer
behind [bɪ'haɪnd]	hinter
bellows ['beləʊz]	Blasebalg
belt [belt]	Gürtel
bench [bentʃ]	Bank
between [bɪ'twiːn]	zwischen
bicycle ['baɪsɪkl]	Fahrrad
big [bɪg]	groß
big wheel [ˌbɪg'wiːl]	Riesenrad
bikini [bɪ'kiːni]	Bikini
bird [bɜːd]	Vogel
biro ['baɪərəʊ]	Kugelschreiber
biscuit ['bɪskɪt]	Keks
black [blæk]	schwarz
blackboard ['blækbɔːd]	Tafel
blanket ['blæŋkɪt]	Decke
blind [blaɪnd]	Rollo
blouse [blaʊz]	Bluse
blue [bluː]	blau
boat [bəʊt]	Boot
bobsleighing ['bɒbsleɪɪŋ]	Bob fahren
body ['bɒdi]	Körper
book [bʊk]	Buch
bookshelf ['bʊkʃelf]	Bücherregal
bookshop ['bʊkʃɒp]	Buchhandlung
boot [buːt]	Stiefel
bottle ['bɒtl]	Flasche
bottom ['bɒtəm]	Po
bowl [bəʊl]	Schüssel
boy [bɔɪ]	Junge
bread [bred]	Brot
break [breɪk]	Pause
brick [brɪk]	Ziegelstein
bridge [brɪdʒ]	Brücke
broom [bruːm]	Besen
brother ['brʌðə]	Bruder
brown [braʊn]	braun
to brush [brʌʃ]	putzen

to brush the teeth [ˌbrʌʃ ðə 'tiːθ]	Zähne putzen
bucket ['bʌkɪt]	Eimer
budgie ['bʌʤi]	Wellensittich
to build [bɪld]	bauen
bumper car ['bʌmpəˌkɑː]	Autoskooter
bus [bʌs]	Bus
bus stop ['bʌsˌstɒp]	Bushaltestelle
bush [bʊʃ]	Busch
busy ['bɪzi]	beschäftigt
but [bʌt, bət]	aber
butcher ['bʊʧə]	Metzger, Metzgerin
butter ['bʌtə]	Butter
butterfly, butterflies ['bʌtəflaɪ]	Schmetterling, Schmetterlinge

C

cage [keɪʤ]	Käfig
cake [keɪk]	Kuchen
calendar ['kæləndə]	Kalender
to call [kɔːl]	rufen
campsite ['kæmpsaɪt]	Zeltplatz
camping stove ['kæmpɪŋ ˌstəʊv]	Gaskocher
can [kæn]	können
candle ['kændl]	Kerze
candy floss ['kændiflɒs]	Zuckerwatte
cap [kæp]	Mütze, Kappe
car [kɑː]	Auto
cardigan ['kɑːdɪgən]	Strickjacke
carpet ['kɑːpɪt]	Teppich
carrier ['kærɪə]	Gepäckträger
carrot ['kærət]	Karotte
to carry ['kæri]	tragen
cartwheel ['kɑːtwiːl]	Rad (Gymnastik)
cat [kæt]	Katze
cauliflower ['kɒlɪflaʊə]	Blumenkohl
CD [ˌsiː'diː]	CD
CD player [ˌsiː'diː ˌpleɪə]	CD-Spieler
chalk [ʧɔːk]	Kreide
chair [ʧeə]	Stuhl
cheek [ʧiːk]	Wange
cheese [ʧiːz]	Käse
chef [ʃef]	Koch, Köchin (Restaurant)
cherry, cherries ['ʧeri]	Kirsche, Kirschen
chest [ʧest]	Brust
chestnut ['ʧesnʌt]	Kastanie (Baum)
chewing gum ['ʧuːɪŋˌgʌm]	Kaugummi
chick [ʧɪk]	Küken
child, children [ʧaɪld], ['ʧɪldrən]	Kind, Kinder
children's room ['ʧɪldrənz ˌruːm]	Kinderzimmer
chimney ['ʧɪmni]	Schornstein
chin ['ʧɪn]	Kinn
chips [ʧɪps]	Pommes frites
chocolate ['ʧɒklət]	Schokolade
Christmas present ['krɪsməs ˌpreznt]	Weihnachtsgeschenk
church [ʧɜːʧ]	Kirche
to clean [kliːn]	putzen
to climb [klaɪm]	klettern
clock [klɒk]	Uhr
closed [kləʊzd]	geschlossen
clothes [kləʊðz]	Kleidung
cloud [klaʊd]	Wolke
cloudy ['klaʊdi]	bewölkt
clown [klaʊn]	Clown
coat [kəʊt]	Mantel
cock [kɒk]	Hahn
cocoa ['kəʊkəʊ]	Kakao
coffee ['kɒfi]	Kaffee
coffee machine ['kɒfi məˌʃiːn]	Kaffeemaschine
coke [kəʊk]	Cola
cold [kəʊld]	kalt
cold [kəʊld]	Schnupfen
cold compress [kəʊld 'kɒmpres]	kalte Kompresse
to collect [kə'lekt]	sammeln
colour ['kʌlə]	Farbe
comb [kəʊm]	Kamm
combine harvester [ˌkɒmbaɪn 'hɑːvɪstə]	Mähdrescher
computer [kəm'pjuːtə]	Computer
conker ['kɒŋkə]	Kastanie (Frucht)
cook [kʊk]	Koch, Köchin
cooker ['kʊkə]	Herd
cooking pots ['kʊkɪŋˌpɒts]	Campinggeschirr
cool bag ['kuːlbæg]	Kühltasche

cough	[kɒf]	Husten
cough medicine	['kɒf ˌmedsɪn]	Hustensaft
cousin	['kʌzn]	Cousine, Cousin
cow	[kaʊ]	Kuh
crocodile	['krɒkədaɪl]	Krokodil
cross-country skiing	[ˌkrɒskʌntri 'ski:ɪŋ]	Skilanglauf
to cry	[kraɪ]	weinen
cucumber	['kju:kʌmbə]	Gurke
cup	[kʌp]	Tasse
cupboard	['kʌbəd]	Schrank
cushion	['kʊʃən]	Kissen
cycling	['saɪklɪŋ]	Radsport

D

to dance	[dɑ:ns]	tanzen
dancer	['dɑ:nsə]	Tänzer, Tänzerin
dancing	['dɑ:nsɪŋ]	Tanzen
daughter	['dɔ:tə]	Tochter
December	[dɪ'sembə]	Dezember
dentist	['dentɪst]	Zahnarzt, Zahnärztin
desk	[desk]	Schreibtisch, Pult
dishcloth	['dɪʃklɒθ]	Geschirrtuch
dishes	['dɪʃɪz]	Geschirr
dishwasher	['dɪʃˌwɒʃə]	Spülmaschine
to dive	[daɪv]	tauchen
diving board	['daɪvɪŋˌbɔ:d]	Sprungbrett
diving ring	['daɪvɪŋˌrɪŋ]	Tauchring
to do	[du:]	tun, machen
to do homework	[ˌdu: 'həʊmwɜ:k]	Hausaufgaben machen
doctor	['dɒktə]	Arzt, Ärztin
dog	[dɒg]	Hund
dog bowl	['dɒgˌbəʊl]	Hundenapf
doll	[dɒl]	Puppe
dolphin	['dɒlfɪn]	Delfin
door	[dɔ:]	Tür
downhill	['daʊnhɪl]	Abfahrt (Ski)
dragon	['drægən]	Drachen
to draw	[drɔ:]	zeichnen
drawer	[drɔ:]	Schublade
to dream	[dri:m]	träumen
dress	[dres]	Kleid
to drink	[drɪŋk]	trinken
duck	[dʌk]	Ente
dunghill	['dʌŋhɪl]	Misthaufen
dustbin	['dʌstbɪn]	Mülleimer
dustpan	['dʌstpæn]	Kehrblech

E

eagle	['i:gl]	Adler
ear	[ɪə]	Ohr
Easter egg	['i:stəˌeg]	Osterei
to eat	[i:t]	essen
egg	[eg]	Ei
elbow	['elbəʊ]	Ellbogen
elephant	['elɪfənt]	Elefant
empty	['empti]	leer
exercise book	['eksəsaɪzˌbʊk]	Heft
eye	[aɪ]	Auge
eyebrow	['aɪbraʊ]	Augenbraue

F

fair	[feə]	Jahrmarkt
family	['fæmɪli]	Familie
farm	[fɑ:m]	Bauernhof
farmer	['fɑ:mə]	Bauer
farmer's wife	[ˌfɑ:məz 'waɪf]	Bäuerin
farmhouse	['fɑ:mhaʊs]	Bauernhaus
farmyard	['fɑ:mjɑ:d]	Hof
fast	[fɑ:st]	schnell
fat	[fæt]	dick
father	['fɑ:ðə]	Vater
feather	['feðə]	Feder
February	['februəri]	Februar
fence	[fens]	Zaun
fever	['fi:və]	Fieber
field	[fi:ld]	Feld
finger	['fɪŋgə]	Finger
fire engine	['faɪəˌrendʒɪn]	Feuerwehrauto
fireman	['faɪəmən]	Feuerwehrmann
firewoman	['faɪəˌwʊmən]	Feuerwehrfrau
fish	[fɪʃ]	Fisch, Fische
flamingo	[flə'mɪŋgəʊ]	Flamingo
floor	[flɔ:]	Fußboden
flower	['flaʊə]	Blume
flu	[flu:]	Grippe
flush	[flʌʃ]	Spülung (Toilette)
to fly	[flaɪ]	fliegen
fly, flies	[flaɪ]	Fliege, Fliegen
foam mattress	['fəʊmˌmætrəs]	Isomatte
fog	[fɒg]	Nebel
foggy	['fɒgi]	neblig

folding chair [ˌfəʊldɪŋ 'tʃeə]	Klappstuhl
folding table [ˌfəʊldɪŋ 'teɪbl]	Klapptisch
food [fu:d]	das Lebensmittel, die Lebensmittel
foot, feet [fʊt], [fi:t]	Fuß, Füße
foot bath ['fʊtbɑ:θ]	Fußbad
football ['fʊtbɔ:l]	Fußball
forehead ['fɔ:hed]	Stirn
fork [fɔ:k]	Gabel
forward roll ['fɔ:wəd ˌrəʊl]	Rolle vorwärts
fox [fɒks]	Fuchs
fracture ['fræktʃə]	Knochenbruch
Friday ['fraɪdeɪ]	Freitag
fridge [frɪdʒ]	Kühlschrank
frosty ['frɒsti]	frostig
fruit [fru:t]	Obst
full [fʊl]	voll

G

garage ['gærɑ:ʒ, 'gærɪdʒ]	Garage
garden ['gɑ:dn]	Garten
gargle ['gɑ:gl]	Gurgelmittel
gate [geɪt]	Tor
to get older [ˌget 'əʊldə]	älter werden
ghost train ['gəʊstˌtreɪn]	Geisterbahn
giraffe [dʒɪ'rɑ:f]	Giraffe
girl [gɜ:l]	Mädchen
to give [gɪv]	geben
glass [glɑ:s]	Glas
glasses ['glɑ:sɪz]	Brille
glove [glʌv]	Handschuh
to go [gəʊ]	gehen
to go for a walk [ˌgəʊ fər ə 'wɔ:k]	spazieren gehen
to go shopping [ˌgəʊ 'ʃɒpɪŋ]	einkaufen gehen
goat [gəʊt]	Ziege
golf [gɒlf]	Golf
grandchild ['grændtʃaɪld]	Enkelkind
grandchildren ['grændtʃɪldrən]	Enkelkinder
grandfather ['grændfɑ:ðə]	Großvater
grandmother ['grændmʌðə]	Großmutter
grape [greɪp]	Weintraube
grass [grɑ:s]	Gras
green [gri:n]	grün
grey [greɪ]	grau
to grow up [ˌgrəʊ 'ʌp]	erwachsen werden
guinea pig ['gɪni ˌpɪg]	Meerschweinchen
gutter ['gʌtə]	Dachrinne
gymnastics [dʒɪm'næstɪks]	Turnen

H

hail [heɪl]	Hagel
to hail [heɪl]	hageln
hair [heə]	Haar
hairbrush ['heəbrʌʃ]	Haarbürste
hairdresser ['heəˌdresə]	Friseur, Friseurin
hair-dryer ['heəˌdraɪə]	Föhn
ham [hæm]	Schinken
hamburger ['hæmˌbɜ:gə]	Hamburger
hammer ['hæmə]	Hammer
hamster ['hæmstə]	Hamster
hand [hænd]	Hand
handkerchief ['hæŋkətʃi:f]	Taschentuch
handlebars ['hændlbɑ:z]	Lenker (Fahrrad)
handstand ['hændstænd]	Handstand
happy ['hæpi]	glücklich
hard [hɑ:d]	hart
hare [heə]	Hase
hat [hæt]	Hut
to have [hæv]	haben
to have got [hæv 'gɒt]	haben
hay [heɪ]	Heu
head [hed]	Kopf
headache ['hedeɪk]	Kopfschmerzen
headstand ['hedstænd]	Kopfstand
to hear [hɪə]	hören
hearing aid ['hɪərɪŋˌeɪd]	Hörgerät
hedge [hedʒ]	Hecke
hedgehog ['hedʒhɒg]	Igel
helicopter ['helɪkɒptə]	Hubschrauber
hen [hen]	Henne
henhouse ['henhaʊs]	Hühnerstall
high [haɪ]	hoch
hiking boots ['haɪkɪŋ ˌbu:ts]	Wanderschuhe
hippo ['hɪpəʊ]	Flusspferd
honey ['hʌni]	Honig
horse [hɔ:s]	Pferd
hospital ['hɒspɪtl]	Krankenhaus
hot [hɒt]	heiß
hot dog ['hɒtdɒg]	Hotdog

hot-water bottle [ˌhɒt'wɔ:təˌbɒtl] Wärmflasche
house [haʊs] Haus
husband ['hʌzbənd] Ehemann

I

ice cream [ˌaɪs'kri:m] Eis
ice hockey [ˌaɪs'hɒki] Eishockey
ice-skating ['aɪsˌskeɪtɪŋ] Eislauf
in front of [ɪn 'frʌnt əv] vor
indicator ['ɪndɪkeɪtə] Anzeige
injection [ɪn'dʒekʃən] Spritze
iron ['aɪən] Bügeleisen
ironing board ['aɪənɪŋˌbɔ:d] Bügelbrett
ivy ['aɪvi] Efeu

J

jacket ['dʒækɪt] Jacke
jam [dʒæm] Marmelade
January ['dʒænuəri] Januar
jeans [dʒi:nz] Jeans
jogging ['dʒɒgɪŋ] Joggen
July [dʒu'laɪ] Juli
to jump [dʒʌmp] springen
jumper ['dʒʌmpə] Pullover
June [dʒu:n] Juni

K

kangaroo [ˌkæŋgə'ru:] Känguru
kennel ['kenl] Hundehütte
to kiss [kɪs] küssen
kitchen ['kɪtʃɪn] Küche
kite [kaɪt] Drachen
knee [ni:] Knie
knee bend ['ni:bend] Kniebeuge
knife [naɪf] Messer
to knock [nɒk] klopfen
to know [nəʊ] wissen, kennen

L

ladder ['lædə] Leiter
ladybird ['leɪdibɜ:d] Marienkäfer
lake [leɪk] See
lamp [læmp] Lampe
to laugh [lɑ:f] lachen
lawn [lɔ:n] Rasen
leaf, leaves [li:f] Blatt, Blätter
left [left] links
leg [leg] Bein
lemon ['lemən] Zitrone
lemonade [ˌlemə'neɪd] Limonade
lesson ['lesən] Unterrichtsstunde
letter box ['letəˌbɒks] Briefkasten
letter boxes ['letəˌbɒksɪz] Briefkästen
lettuce ['letɪs] Salat
life belt ['laɪfbelt] Rettungsring
lightning ['laɪtnɪŋ] Blitz
to like [laɪk] mögen
lilo ['laɪləʊ] Luftmatratze
lion ['laɪən] Löwe
to listen ['lɪsn] zuhören
living room ['lɪvɪŋrʊm] Wohnzimmer
long [lɒŋ] lang
to look [lʊk] schauen
to look for ['lʊk fɔ:] suchen
loud [laʊd] laut
lorry ['lɒri] LKW
loudspeaker [ˌlaʊd'spi:kə] Lautsprecher
low [ləʊ] niedrig
lunch [lʌntʃ] Mittagessen

M

magazine [ˌmægə'zi:n] Zeitschrift
to make [meɪk] machen
man [mæn] Mann
manager ['mænɪdʒə] Manager
map [mæp] Landkarte
March [mɑ:tʃ] März
May [meɪ] Mai
microwave ['maɪkrəʊweɪv] Mikrowelle
milk [mɪlk] Milch
mirror ['mɪrə] Spiegel
mittens ['mɪtnz] Fäustlinge
mobile phone [ˌməʊbaɪl 'fəʊn] Handy
Monday ['mʌndeɪ] Montag
monkey ['mʌŋki] Affe
mother ['mʌðə] Mutter
motorbike ['məʊtəbaɪk] Motorrad
mouse [maʊs] Maus
mouth [maʊθ] Mund
museum [mju:'zi:əm] Museum
mushrooms ['mʌʃrʊmz] Pilze

N

neck [nek] Hals
to need [ni:d] brauchen
newspaper ['nju:zˌpeɪpə] Zeitung
next to ['nekst tu:] neben
nightdress ['naɪtdres] Nachthemd
nose [nəʊz] Nase

November [nəʊ'vembə]	November
number ['nʌmbə]	Zahl, Nummer
nurse [nɜ:s]	Krankenschwester

O

October [ɒk'təʊbə]	Oktober
oil [ɔɪl]	Öl
ointment ['ɔɪntmənt]	Salbe
old [əʊld]	alt
on [ɒn]	auf
one-leg stand [ˌwʌnleg 'stænd]	Waage (Sport)
open ['əʊpən]	geöffnet
opposite ['ɒpəzɪt]	Gegenteil, Gegensatz
orange ['ɒrɪndʒ]	Orange, orange
orange juice ['ɒrɪndʒˌdʒu:s]	Orangensaft
oven ['ʌvn]	Backofen
oven cloth ['ʌvnklɒθ]	Topflappen
over ['əʊvə]	über

P

to paint [peɪnt]	malen
painter and decorator ['peɪntər ənd 'dekəreɪtə]	Maler(in) und Anstreicher(in)
pan [pæn]	Pfanne
pants [pænts]	Unterhose
paper ['peɪpə]	Papier
parents ['peərənts]	Eltern
parrot ['pærət]	Papagei
part [pɑ:t]	Teil
pasture ['pɑ:stʃə]	Weide
pavement ['peɪvmənt]	Bürgersteig
peach [pi:tʃ]	Pfirsich
peacock ['pi:kɒk]	Pfau
pear [peə]	Birne
peas [pi:z]	Erbsen
pen [pen]	Füller
pencil ['pensl]	Bleistift
pencil case ['penslˌkeɪs]	Mäppchen
pencil sharpener ['penslˌʃɑ:pnə]	Anspitzer
penguin ['peŋgwɪn]	Pinguin
pepper ['pepə]	Pfeffer
petrol station ['petrəlˌsteɪʃn]	Tankstelle
to pick [pɪk]	pflücken
picture ['pɪktʃə]	Bild
picture book ['pɪktʃəˌbʊk]	Bilderbuch
pig [pɪg]	Schwein
pillow ['pɪləʊ]	Kopfkissen
pineapple ['paɪnæpl]	Ananas
pink [pɪŋk]	rosa
pitchfork ['pɪtʃfɔ:k]	Mistgabel
plant [plɑ:nt]	Pflanze
plaster ['plɑ:stə]	Gips, Pflaster
plastic flower [ˌplæstik 'flaʊə]	Plastikblume
plate [pleɪt]	Teller
to play [pleɪ]	spielen
playpen ['pleɪpen]	Laufstall
please [pli:z]	bitte
plum [plʌm]	Pflaume
polar bear ['pəʊləˌbeə]	Eisbär
police car [pə'li:sˌkɑ:]	Polizeiauto
policeman [pə'li:smən]	Polizist
policewoman [pə'li:sˌwʊmən]	Polizistin
pond [pɒnd]	Teich
pool [pu:l]	Becken
popcorn ['pɒpkɔ:n]	Popcorn
post office ['pəʊstˌɒfɪs]	Postamt
poster ['pəʊstə]	Poster
postman ['pəʊstmən]	Postbote
pot [pɒt]	Topf
potato, potatoes [pə'teɪtəʊ], [pə'teɪtəʊz]	Kartoffel, Kartoffeln
pound [paʊnd]	Pfund
profession [prə'feʃən]	Beruf
programmer ['prəʊgræmə]	Programmierer
pub [pʌb]	Kneipe
to pull [pʊl]	ziehen
pupil ['pju:pl]	Schüler
puppet ['pʌpɪt]	Handpuppe
puppet theatre ['pʌpɪtˌθɪətə]	Puppentheater
purple ['pɜ:pl]	lila
to push [pʊʃ]	drücken
pyjamas [pɪ'dʒɑ:məz]	Schlafanzug

Q

quiet ['kwaɪət]	leise

R

rabbit ['ræbɪt]	Kaninchen
radiator ['reɪdieɪtə]	Heizung
radio ['reɪdiəʊ]	Radio
rain [reɪn]	Regen
to rain [reɪn]	regnen

raincoat ['reɪnkəʊt]	Regenmantel
rainy ['reɪni]	regnerisch
to read [ri:d]	lesen
red [red]	rot
red pepper [ˌred 'pepə]	roter Paprika
remote control [rɪˌməʊt kən'trəʊl]	Fernbedienung
rhino ['raɪnəʊ]	Nashorn
riding ['raɪdɪŋ]	Reiten
right [raɪt]	rechts, richtig
ring [rɪŋ]	Ring
river ['rɪvə]	Fluss
roller coaster ['rəʊləˌkəʊstə]	Achterbahn
roof [ru:f]	Dach
rope [rəʊp]	Leine, Seil
rose [rəʊz]	Rose
roundabout ['raʊndəˌbaʊt]	Karussell
to row [rəʊ]	rudern
rowing ['rəʊɪŋ]	Rudern
rubber ['rʌbə]	Gummi, Radiergummi
rubber boot ['rʌbəˌbu:t]	Gummistiefel
rubber duck ['rʌbəˌdʌk]	Gummiente
rubber ring ['rʌbəˌrɪŋ]	Schwimmring
rubbish bin ['rʌbɪʃˌbɪn]	Mülleimer
rucksack ['rʌksæk]	Rucksack
ruler ['ru:lə]	Lineal
to run [rʌn]	rennen
S	
sad [sæd]	traurig
saddle ['sædl]	Sattel
sailing ['seɪlɪŋ]	Segeln
salt [sɔ:lt]	Salz
sand [sænd]	Sand
sandals ['sændlz]	Sandalen
sandpit ['sændpɪt]	Sandkasten
satchel ['sætʃl]	Schultasche
saucer ['sɔ:sə]	Untertasse
sauna ['sɔ:nə]	Sauna
sausage ['sɒsɪdʒ]	Würstchen
saxophone ['sæksəfəʊn]	Saxophon
scarf [skɑ:f]	Schal
school [sku:l]	Schule
school uniform [ˌsku:l 'ju:nɪfɔ:m]	Schuluniform
scissors ['sɪzəz]	Schere, Scheren

season ['si:zn]	Jahreszeit
to see [si:]	sehen
seesaw ['si:sɔ:]	Wippe
sentence ['sentəns]	Satz
September [sep'tembə]	September
sheep [ʃi:p]	Schaf, Schafe
shoes [ʃu:z]	Schuhe
shop [ʃɒp]	Geschäft
shopping centre ['ʃɒpɪŋˌsentə]	Einkaufszentrum
short [ʃɔ:t]	kurz
shorts [ʃɔ:ts]	Shorts
shoulder ['ʃəʊldə]	Schulter
to shout [ʃaʊt]	rufen
to show [ʃəʊ]	zeigen
shower ['ʃaʊə]	Dusche
shower curtain ['ʃaʊəˌkɜ:tn]	Duschvorhang
shower gel ['ʃaʊəˌdʒel]	Duschgel
to sing [sɪŋ]	singen
singer ['sɪŋə]	Sänger, Sängerin
sink [sɪŋk]	Spüle
sister ['sɪstə]	Schwester
to sit [sɪt]	sitzen
skating ['skeɪtɪŋ]	Skaten
skiing ['ski:ɪŋ]	Ski fahren
skipping rope ['skɪpɪŋrəʊp]	Hüpfseil
skirt [skɜ:t]	Rock
sky [skaɪ]	Himmel
to sleep [sli:p]	schlafen
sleeping bag ['sli:pɪŋˌbæg]	Schlafsack
slide [slaɪd]	Rutsche
slippers ['slɪpəz]	Hausschuhe
slow [sləʊ]	langsam
small [smɔ:l]	klein
to smile [smaɪl]	lächeln
snake [sneɪk]	Schlange
snow [snəʊ]	Schnee
to snow [snəʊ]	schneien
snowboarding ['snəʊbɔ:dɪŋ]	Snowboarden
snowman ['snəʊmæn]	Schneemann
snowy ['snəʊi]	verschneit

soap [səʊp]	Seife
soccer ['sɒkə]	Fußball
socket ['sɒkɪt]	Steckdose
socks [sɒks]	Socken
sofa ['səʊfə]	Sofa
soft [sɒft]	weich
solarium [səʊ'leəriəm]	Solarium
son [sʌn]	Sohn
sore throat [ˌsɔː 'θrəʊt]	Halsschmerzen
spade [speɪd]	Schaufel, Schippe
spider ['spaɪdə]	Spinne
spider's web ['spaɪdəzˌweb]	Spinnennetz
sponge [spʌnʤ]	Schwamm
spoon [spuːn]	Löffel
sport [spɔːt]	Sport
spots [spɒts]	Pickel
to sprain [spreɪn]	verstauchen
spring [sprɪŋ]	Frühling
squirrel ['skwɪrəl]	Eichhörnchen
stable ['steɪbl]	Stall
stairs [steəz]	Treppe, Stufen
starting block ['stɑːtɪŋˌblɒk]	Startblock
stomach ['stʌmək]	Bauch, Magen
stomach ache ['stʌməkˌeɪk]	Bauchschmerzen
stone [stəʊn]	Stein
storm [stɔːm]	Sturm
stormy ['stɔːmi]	stürmisch
straw [strɔː]	Stroh
strawberry ['strɔːbəri]	Erdbeere
sugar ['ʃʊgə]	Zucker
suit [suːt]	Anzug
summer ['sʌmə]	Sommer
sun [sʌn]	Sonne
sun lounger ['sʌnˌlaʊnʤə]	Sonnenliege
sunflower ['sʌnflaʊə]	Sonnenblume
sunny ['sʌni]	sonnig
sunshade ['sʌnʃeɪd]	Sonnenschirm
supermarket ['suːpəˌmɑːkɪt]	Supermarkt
surfing ['sɜːfɪŋ]	Surfen
sweetcorn ['swiːtkɔːn]	Mais
to swim [swɪm]	schwimmen
swimming ['swɪmɪŋ]	Schwimmen
swimming pool ['swɪmɪŋˌpuːl]	Schwimmbad
swimming trunks ['swɪmɪŋˌtrʌŋks]	Badehose
swimsuit ['swɪmsuːt]	Badeanzug
to swing [swɪŋ]	schaukeln

T

table ['teɪbl]	Tisch
tablet ['tæblɪt]	Tablette
tailor ['teɪlə]	Schneider, Schneiderin
to take [teɪk]	nehmen
to talk [tɔːk]	reden
tap [tæp]	Wasserhahn
tea [tiː]	Tee
teacher ['tiːʧə]	Lehrer, Lehrerin
teddy bear ['tediˌbeə]	Teddybär
telephone ['telɪfəʊn]	Telefon
television ['telɪvɪʒən]	Fernsehen
temperature ['temprɪʧə]	Temperatur
tennis ['tenɪs]	Tennis
tent [tent]	Zelt
tent peg ['tentpeg]	Hering (Zelt)
thank you ['θæŋk juː]	danke
there [ðeə]	dort
thermometer [θə'mɒmɪtə]	Thermometer
thermos flask ['θɜːmɒsˌflɑːsk]	Thermoskanne
thin [θɪn]	dünn
thing [θɪŋ]	Sache, Ding
to think [θɪŋk]	denken
thumb [θʌm]	Daumen
thunder ['θʌndə]	Donner
thunderstorm ['θʌndəˌstɔːm]	Gewitter
Thursday ['θɜːzdeɪ]	Donnerstag
ticket ['tɪkɪt]	Los, Eintrittskarte
tie [taɪ]	Krawatte
tiger ['taɪgə]	Tiger
tights [taɪts]	Strumpfhose
tile [taɪl]	Fliese
time [taɪm]	Zeit
timetable ['taɪmˌteɪbl]	Stundenplan
tin [tɪn]	Konservendose
toad [təʊd]	Kröte

today [tə'deɪ]	heute
toe [təʊ]	Zeh
toilet ['tɔɪlət]	Toilette
toilet paper ['tɔɪlət,peɪpə]	Toilettenpapier
tomato, tomatoes [tə'mɑːtəʊ]	Tomate, Tomaten
tooth, teeth [tuːθ], [tiːθ]	Zahn, Zähne
toothache ['tuːθeɪk]	Zahnschmerzen
toothbrush ['tuːθbrʌʃ]	Zahnbürste
toothpaste ['tuːθpeɪst]	Zahncreme
torch [tɔːtʃ]	Taschenlampe
towel [taʊəl]	Handtuch
tower [taʊə]	Turm
town [taʊn]	Stadt
toy [tɔɪ]	Spielzeug
toy car ['tɔɪ ˌkɑː]	Spielzeugauto
tractor ['træktə]	Traktor
traffic lights ['træfɪk,laɪts]	Ampel
traffic sign ['træfɪk,saɪn]	Verkehrsschild
trainers ['treɪnəz]	Turnschuhe
tree [triː]	Baum
trousers ['traʊzəz]	Hose
Tuesday ['tjuːzdeɪ]	Dienstag
turtle ['tɜːtl]	Schildkröte
tyre ['taɪə]	Reifen

U

umbrella [ʌm'brelə]	Regenschirm
uncle ['ʌŋkl]	Onkel
under ['ʌndə]	unter

V

vase [vɑːz]	Vase
very ['veri]	sehr
vest [vest]	Unterhemd
vinegar ['vɪnɪgə]	Essig
vocabulary [vəʊ'kæbjʊləri]	Vokabeln
volleyball ['vɒlibɔːl]	Volleyball

W

to wait [weɪt]	warten
to walk [wɔːk]	gehen
to want [wɒnt]	wollen, möchten
wardrobe ['wɔːdrəʊb]	Schrank
warm [wɔːm]	warm
water ['wɔːtə]	Wasser
watering can ['wɔːtərɪŋkæn]	Gießkanne
water skiing ['wɔːtə,skiːɪŋ]	Wasserski
water slide ['wɔːtəslaɪd]	Wasserrutsche
water wings ['wɔːtəwɪŋz]	Schwimmflügel
weather ['weðə]	Wetter
Wednesday ['wenzdeɪ]	Mittwoch
weightlifting ['weɪt,lɪftɪŋ]	Gewichtheben
wellington boots [ˌwelɪŋtən 'buːts]	Gummistiefel
wet [wet]	nass
what [wɒt]	was
wheel [wiːl]	Rad
wheelbarrow ['wiːl,bærəʊ]	Schubkarre
when [wen]	wenn
where [weə]	wo
to whisper ['wɪspə]	flüstern
who [huː]	wer
wife [waɪf]	Ehefrau
wind [wɪnd]	Wind
window ['wɪndəʊ]	Fenster
windowsill ['wɪndəʊsɪl]	Fensterbank
windy ['wɪndi]	windig
winter ['wɪntə]	Winter
wolf, wolves [wʊlf]	Wolf
woman ['wʊmən]	Frau
worm [wɜːm]	Wurm
wound [waʊnd]	Wunde
to write [raɪt]	schreiben

Y

year [jɪə]	Jahr
yellow ['jeləʊ]	gelb
young [jʌŋ]	jung

Z

zebra ['zebrə]	Zebra
zip [zɪp]	Reißverschluss